I0616883

40 Days of Thought Therapy

Changing Our Thinking to God's Way of Thinking

By

Bishop Thomas Thompson Jr.

40 Days of Thought Therapy: Changing Our Thinking to God's Way of Thinking

Written by Bishop Thomas Thompson Jr.

Published by:

YOUNSPIRE PUBLISHING

ISBN: 979-8-9923903-0-8

Table of Contents

Introduction

"As a Man Thinketh in His Heart, So Is He"

Proverbs 23:7

Welcome to **40 Days of Thought Therapy**, a journey of changing our thinking to align with God's way of thinking. This devotional is more than just a collection of reflections; it's an invitation to embark on a transformational journey to renew your mind and align your heart with the character of God.

Our thoughts are powerful—they shape our lives, direct our actions, and influence our outcomes. As Proverbs 23:7 reminds us, "As a man thinketh in his heart, so is he." What we dwell on in our minds becomes our reality, whether positive or negative. This book is designed to help you take control of your thought life by immersing yourself in God's truth, renewing your perspective, and stepping into the prophetic possibilities He has prepared for you.

The Battle of the Mind

The thoughts and inclinations of the heart shape our reality. When we think about our problems, they are magnified. But when we think about God's provision, His answers become magnified.

Our thoughts have the ability to limit or liberate us.

> ***"Your thoughts don't have to be true to hurt you; you just have to believe them."***
>
> *Prophet T.G. Thompson*

"Be careful how you think; your life is shaped by your thoughts." I remember speaking with my dad and he shared with me in one of our private sessions, he said Junior "Your thoughts don't have to be true to hurt you; you just have to believe them. If you tell

yourself your marriage won't last, then it won't. If you're afraid you can't do something, then you won't. Your thoughts run your life! Your circumstances may be out of your control, but God is in control of everything.

If you feed your mind with fear, failure, and negativity, you will see those results. But if you choose God's thoughts—His Word and promises—your life will begin to reflect His divine plan for you.

Preface

As I pen these words, my heart is filled with gratitude for the journey that has led to the creation of *40 Days of Thought Therapy: Changing Our Thinking to God's Way of Thinking.* This book is not just a compilation of lessons, but a reflection of my personal walk with God—a journey marked by trials, triumphs, and an unshakable reliance on His promises.

The mind is a battlefield, and every believer faces challenges in aligning their thoughts with God's truth. Over the years, I have witnessed countless individuals myself included, struggle with negative thinking, worry, and doubt. Through the transformative power of God's Word, I have come to understand that renewing the mind is the key to overcoming these obstacles and stepping into God's divine purpose.

This 40-day journey was birthed out of a deep desire to provide practical tools and spiritual insight for those seeking freedom from the limitations of negative thinking. Each day is designed to guide you through a process of reflection, renewal, and restoration. The scriptures, prayers, and lessons within these pages are meant to challenge your thinking, inspire your faith, and draw you closer to God.

My prayer is that this book will be more than just a read—it will be an experience. May it serve as a roadmap for your transformation, equipping you to think, speak, and live according to God's Word. Remember, the life you desire begins with the thoughts you cultivate. As Proverbs 23:7 reminds us, "As a man thinketh in his heart, so is he."

I am humbled by the opportunity to walk this journey with you, and I trust that God will meet you in every moment of reflection and prayer. May you emerge from this journey with a renewed mind, a strengthened spirit, and a deeper connection to the One who holds your destiny.

With God's peace and love,

Bishop Thomas Thompson Jr.

Foreword

It is with great honor and deep admiration that I write this foreword for *40 Days of Thought Therapy: Changing Our Thinking to God's Way of Thinking.* This transformative book, written by Bishop Thomas Thompson Jr., is a masterpiece of wisdom, spiritual guidance, and practical strategies for renewing the mind. Bishop Thompson has poured his heart and soul into these pages, crafting a 40-day journey that is both deeply personal and universally impactful.

As believers, we understand the battlefield of the mind is where victories are won or lost. Bishop Thompson's profound insights remind us that our thoughts shape our reality and direct our destiny. He expertly weaves scriptural truths with practical applications, empowering readers to confront and conquer negative thinking, worry, and doubt. Each day is a step closer to the mind of Christ, enabling us to embrace the abundant life God has planned for us.

Having had the privilege of knowing Bishop Thompson, his life is a testament to the principles he shares in this book. Through seasons of triumph and trial, he has exemplified unwavering faith and reliance on God's promises. This book reflects that same faith, offering readers a roadmap to healing, transformation, and victory.

I encourage you to approach this 40-day journey with an open heart and expectant spirit. Let these pages inspire, challenge, and equip you for a renewed mindset and a deeper relationship with God. By the end of this journey, I am confident you will not only think differently but live differently, walking in alignment with God's purpose for your life.

Prepare to be transformed. This is not just a book; it is a divine encounter.

In His Service,

Dr. Joy Riley

Dedication

This book is dedicated to empowering believers to align their thoughts with God's Word, fostering spiritual growth, clarity, and transformation. It is written for everyone engaged in a battle of the mind, whether financially, physically, mentally, or spiritually. To those seeking peace, purpose, and victory, this book is for you. May it be a guiding light that leads you to triumph through the renewing power of God's truth.

Acknowledgments

This book was made possible through the love, prayers, and support of many special people and family members. First and foremost, I want to acknowledge my Lord and Savior Jesus Christ for empowering me with creative power and purpose to transform hearts and minds through the revelation of His will and Word.

To my father, Dr. T.G. Thompson Sr., who taught me invaluable lessons about faith, resilience, and the power of God's thoughts. He demonstrated unwavering trust in God's plan, even through life's toughest battles, leaving a legacy of strength and faith.

To my mother, Mother Martha Thompson, whose life of selfless love, prayer, and generosity continues to inspire me daily. She is a beacon of God's grace and perseverance.

To my wife, Prophetess Lorraine Thompson, my pillar of strength, joy, and encouragement. You exemplify a Proverbs 31 woman, and your unwavering faith in both good and challenging times has been a source of inspiration and grounding for me. I am forever grateful for your prayers, sacrifices, and love.

To my daughters, Ebony and Essence, thank you for your unconditional support and belief in me, especially during challenging seasons. Your love has been a light in my life.

To the Gospel Arena International Ministry of Miami, I thank you for your trust, loyalty, and partnership as we follow God together.

Lastly, to Dr. Joy Riley, whose integrity, expertise, and guidance have been instrumental in bringing this book to life. Thank you for your dedication and passion in helping others.

Word of Impartation from the Author

God is calling us to a higher place of understanding and discernment—a Kingdom perspective that aligns with His divine wisdom. No longer are we to live by cultural norms, traditions, emotions, or human reasoning. Instead, we must anchor our decisions and actions in God's thoughts and His Word.

The psalmist prayed, *"I am your servant; give me understanding, so that I may know your decrees"* (Psalm 119:125). Similarly, my prayer for you is that this book will help you understand God's wisdom and renew your mind according to His truth.

As we renew our minds through His Word, we align ourselves with His divine plan. This transformation leads to righteousness, peace, and joy in the Holy Spirit. It allows us to see beyond our circumstances and embrace the abundant life He has for us.

One of the greatest moments in life is when we fully surrender to God and trust His plan. Renewing our minds is not a one-time event but a daily journey of choosing to think and act according to His truth. It is my hope that the lessons and reflections in this book will inspire you to partner with the Holy Spirit, set your mind on things above, and live a transformed life.

The Purpose:
Renewing the Mind for Transformation

The purpose of this devotional is to guide you into a deeper understanding of the role your thoughts play in your spiritual, emotional, and even physical well-being. Your thoughts are not random; they are electrical impulses that impact every decision, word, action, and reaction. Yet, they can be changed, reoriented, and aligned with the Word of God.

Paul's encouragement in **Romans 12:2** serves as the foundation of this journey:

"Do not conform to the pattern of this world, but be transformed by the renewing of your mind."

God calls us to think His thoughts, to operate with His wisdom, and to reflect His character in every area of our lives. By doing so, we can walk in purpose, peace, and victory.

A Journey of A 40 Days Devotional

This devotional unfolds over 40 days, offering practical tools, reflective questions, scripture-based affirmations, and powerful prayers to guide your thought life. Each day builds on the last, creating a steady process of renewal:

1. **Begin with Awareness:** Understand the current state of your thought life and how it shapes your actions.

2. **Replace Lies with Truth:** Identify negative, limiting beliefs and replace them with God's promises.

3. **Declare Prophetic Possibilities:** Speak God's truth over your life, believing for transformation.

4. **Step Into God's Plan:** Boldly align your actions with the renewed mindset God has given you.

The Spiritual Foundation: Prophetic Possibility Thinking

Becoming a prophetic thinker means allowing God's Word to shape your thoughts, influence your actions, and direct your destiny. It means seeing beyond what is and stepping into what God has declared possible.

The Transformative Process

To become prophetic thinkers, we must adopt God's way of thinking and live with a **prophetic mindset**. As it says in Isaiah 55:8-9:

"For my thoughts are not your thoughts, neither are your ways my ways," declares the Lord. "As the heavens are higher than the earth, so are my ways higher than your ways and my thoughts than your thoughts."

Prophetic possibility thinking is rooted in understanding and trusting God's higher ways. It's about learning to see yourself, your circumstances, and your future through God's eyes. When you adopt this mindset, you begin to declare God's promises with boldness, shaping your reality with the power of His Word.

In essence of this process of allowing God to change the way we think is not easy, but it is essential. Through this process, we unlock what has held us back relationally, professionally, and spiritually

What to Expect:
Heart Work, Not Just Head Knowledge

This journey requires more than intellectual understanding; Psalm 19:14 says, *"Let the words of my mouth and the meditation of my heart be acceptable in Your sight, O Lord, my Rock and my Redeemer."*

Our relationship with God requires **heart work**: slowing down, admitting our real thoughts, and aligning our hearts with Him. When our thoughts and words match the content of our hearts, we speak with power, authenticity, and divine alignment. That is why Proverbs 23:7 shows us that we must be concerns about the content of our hearts because it truly matters a lot to God.

What we think about and believe in our hearts matters greatly to God because it reflects who we truly are. One of the most amazing gifts that God has given us the human mind. The ability to learn, think, choose, and reason is the essence of what makes us human.

God doesn't just want you to think good thoughts—He desires transformation from the inside out. That transformation begins when your thoughts, words, and actions align with His truth. This process includes:

- **Replacing Negative Thoughts:** Counter lies with scripture and affirmations that reflect God's promises.

- **Speaking Life:** Declaring His Word boldly over every area of your life.

- **Meditating on Scripture:** Allowing His Word to dwell richly in your heart and mind.

- **Engaging in Prophetic Action:** Acting in faith, trusting that His plans for you are good.

Are you wondering why 40 Days?

The number 40 holds spiritual significance in scripture—it represents periods of testing, preparation, and transformation. Moses spent 40 days on Mount Sinai receiving God's commandments. Jesus fasted for 40 days in the wilderness, preparing for His ministry. Similarly, these 40 days will be a time of spiritual renewal and preparation for the next phase of your journey with God.

What You'll Gain

By the end of this devotional, you will have:

- A renewed mind that aligns with God's truth.

- A deeper understanding of how your thoughts influence your destiny.

- Practical tools to combat negative thinking and replace it with prophetic possibilities.

- Confidence to speak and live in alignment with God's promises.

Your Invitation

God is inviting you to step into His thoughts, His ways, and His plans for your life. He wants to equip you to overcome every challenge, walk boldly in your purpose, and experience the fullness of His promises.

Take these next 40 days seriously. Commit to the process, and let God revolutionize your life through the power of thought therapy. As you embark on this journey, remember this truth:

You have the power to transform your life by transforming your thoughts.

Let us begin this journey of thought renewal with open hearts, surrendered minds, and the expectation that God will do exceedingly, abundantly above all we can ask or imagine.

The Spirit of Excellence is not a skill; it is an **attitude**. Your thoughts determine your character, and your character determines your future. As Williams James once said:

"The greatest discovery of my generation is that human beings can alter their lives by altering their attitude of mind."

God's plan for your life is for you to **prosper**—not just financially, but spiritually, emotionally, and mentally. By renewing your mind with His Word, you will:

- Discover who you are in Christ.
- Unlock His divine purpose for your life.
- Overcome limiting beliefs that have held you back.

As Romans 12:2 declares: *"Do not conform to the pattern of this world but be transformed by the renewing of your mind."*

Let's Began with a simple prayer.

Father, thank You for the gift of this journey. I surrender my thoughts to You and ask that You transform my mind through Your Word. Teach me to see myself and my circumstances through Your eyes. Help me to embrace Your promises and walk boldly into the destiny You have prepared for me. In Jesus' name, Amen.

Day 1:
The Power of Positive Thinking

Focus Scripture: *"I can do all things through Christ who strengthens me."* — Philippians 4:13 (KJV)

Thought Therapy Lesson The words we speak become the house we live in. Begin to speak life over every area of your life. Speak life over your finances, your children, your health, and your dreams. God's Word reminds us that our strength is renewed as we place our hope in Him (Isaiah 40:31). Today, choose to align your thoughts and speech with God's truth rather than the negativity of the world.

- **Reflection:** What area of your life feels "dry" or lifeless? How can you begin to speak God's promises into that area?

- **Practical Step:** Write down 3 affirmations based on Scripture and speak them aloud throughout the day. Example: "I am strong and courageous because God is with me" (Joshua 1:9).

Questions

1. **Why is it important to focus on God's perspective about our lives?**

- Answer: Focusing on God's perspective helps us remain joyful and trust in His plans, even during challenges (Philippians 4:13).

2. **How does positive speech affect our lives?**

- Answer: Speaking life aligns us with God's promises, bringing renewal and transformation (Isaiah 40:31).

3. **Who empowers us to live out God's purpose?**

- Answer: The Holy Spirit enables us to live and think in alignment with God's Word (1 Corinthians 2:16).

Declaration Prayer: Heavenly Father, I thank You for renewing my strength today. I declare that I can do all things through Christ who strengthens me. Let my words reflect Your promises, and may they bring life to every area of my being. I trust in You to guide and sustain me. In Jesus' name, Amen.

Glossary Word:

Renewal

- Definition: The process of becoming new or revived through the power of God.

Day 2:
Stop Looking Back

Focus Scripture: *"Finally, brothers and sisters, whatever is true, whatever is noble, whatever is right, whatever is pure, whatever is lovely, whatever is admirable—if anything is excellent or praiseworthy—think about such things."* — Philippians 4:8 (NIV)

Thought Therapy Lesson Stop dwelling on what you think you've lost and start focusing on what God has in store for you. Replace negative thoughts with God's truth. Transformation comes when we allow the Word of God to shape our thinking. You are a person of value because God values you deeply.

- **Reflection:** Are there thoughts from your past that are hindering your growth? How can you surrender them to God today?

- **Practical Step:** Write down a "loss" you've been dwelling on and ask God to reveal the new blessings He's bringing into your life.

Questions

1. **What does Philippians 4:8 teach us about our thought life?**

- Answer: It encourages us to focus on positive, godly things that uplift our spirit and align us with Christ.

2. **How can transformation occur through God's Word?**

- Answer: By meditating on and applying God's truth, our thoughts and actions begin to reflect His character (Romans 12:2).

3. **What makes us valuable in God's eyes?**

- Answer: Our worth comes from being created in His image and redeemed through Christ (Genesis 1:27).

Declaration Prayer Lord, I release my past to You and embrace the future You have prepared for me. Help me to think on things that are true, noble, and praiseworthy. I trust in Your plans for my life and declare that transformation is taking place in my mind and heart. In Jesus' name, Amen.

Glossary Word:

Transformation

- Definition: A complete change in a person's thoughts and actions, aligning them with God's purpose.

Day 3:
Capturing Every Thought

Focus Scripture: *"We demolish arguments and every pretension that sets itself up against the knowledge of God, and we take captive every thought to make it obedient to Christ."* — 2 Corinthians 10:5 (NIV)

Thought Therapy Lesson Your mind is a battlefield, and the enemy seeks to plant seeds of doubt and fear. However, God has given you authority to take captive every thought and make it obedient to Christ. Today, choose to reject negative thoughts and replace them with God's truth.

- **Reflection:** Are there recurring thoughts that don't align with God's Word? How can you address them today?

- **Practical Step:** Identify one negative thought and write a Scripture-based truth to counteract it. For example, replace "I am not enough" with "I am fearfully and wonderfully made" (Psalm 139:14).

Questions

1. **What does it mean to take a thought captive?**

- Answer: It means to consciously align our thoughts with God's Word and reject those that oppose His truth.

2. **Why is it important to address negative thoughts?**

- Answer: Negative thoughts can lead to actions that stray from God's purpose (James 1:14-15).

3. **How does God's Word help us overcome negative thinking?**

- Answer: Scripture provides truth and guidance to replace lies and align our minds with God's will (Ephesians 6:17).

Declaration Prayer Father, I take captive every thought that does not align with Your Word. I declare that my mind is renewed, and I am focused on Your truth. Strengthen me to reject lies and stand firm in Your promises. In Jesus' name, Amen.

Glossary Word:

Obedience

- Definition: Submission to God's authority and alignment with His Word.

Day 4:
Worry-Free Living

Focus Scripture: *"Cast all your anxiety on him because he cares for you."* — 1 Peter 5:7 (NIV)

Thought Therapy Lesson Worrying robs us of peace and joy. Anxiety causes us to question God's faithfulness, but He reminds us to cast our cares upon Him. God cares deeply about you and your needs. Today, release every worry to the Lord and trust that He is working everything out for your good.

- **Reflection:** What worries are weighing you down? How can you lay them at God's feet today?

- **Practical Step:** Write a prayer of surrender, listing each worry or burden you are carrying. Afterward, declare that you trust God to handle them.

Questions

1. **What does 1 Peter 5:7 teach us about God's care for us?**

- Answer: It shows that God is deeply concerned about our well-being and wants us to trust Him with our burdens.

2. **Why is worry counterproductive?**

- Answer: Worry distracts us from God's promises and does not change our circumstances (Matthew 6:27).

3. **What happens when we cast our anxieties on God?**

- Answer: We experience His peace and assurance that He is in control (Philippians 4:6-7).

Declaration Prayer Father, I cast all my cares and anxieties on You, knowing that You care for me. I release every worry and trust in Your perfect plan. Thank You for Your peace and provision. In Jesus' name, Amen.

Glossary Word:

Anxiety

- Definition: A feeling of worry or unease, often about the future, that can be overcome through trust in God.

Day 5:
Overcoming Negative Thoughts

Focus Scripture: *"Count it all joy, my brothers, when you meet trials of various kinds."* — James 1:2 (ESV)

Thought Therapy Lesson God's plan for your life is bigger than the obstacles you face. Don't let negative thoughts convince you otherwise. When trials come, count it all joy, knowing that God is building your character and strengthening your faith. Declare today that you are an overcomer through Christ.

- **Reflection:** How can you view your current challenges as opportunities for growth?

- **Practical Step:** Write down one trial you are currently facing and list three ways God might use it for your good.

Questions

1. **Why does James encourage us to count trials as joy?**

- Answer: Trials produce endurance, character, and hope in our lives (Romans 5:3-5).

2. **What role does faith play in overcoming negativity?**

- Answer: Faith shifts our perspective, helping us see God's greater purpose in every situation (2 Corinthians 5:7).

3. **What promise does God provide in trials?**

- Answer: He promises to never leave or forsake us and to work all things together for our good (Romans 8:28).

Declaration Prayer Lord, I thank You for turning my trials into opportunities for growth. I count it all joy, knowing that You are working in my life. Help me to trust in Your process and find strength in Your promises. In Jesus' name, Amen.

Glossary Word:

Endurance

- Definition: The ability to persevere through trials and challenges while trusting in God's strength and guidance.

Day 6:
Rest in God's Strength

Focus Scripture: *"Come to me, all who labor and are heavy laden, and I will give you rest."* — Matthew 11:28 (ESV)

Thought Therapy Lesson The burdens we carry are not meant to overwhelm us. Jesus invites us to find rest in Him. Today, shift your focus from self-reliance to God-dependence. Release the weight of your struggles to Him and allow His peace to fill your heart.

We often try to handle life's challenges alone, believing we must carry every weight, decision, and difficulty on our own shoulders. Yet Jesus assures us that His yoke is easy, and His burden is light (Matthew 11:30). When we surrender our struggles to Him, we exchange stress for peace, weariness for rest, and weakness for strength. God never intended for us to bear these loads alone.

True rest begins in the soul—it's not just physical relief, but a spiritual renewal. As you rest in God's presence, you will feel His peace wash over you, assuring you that He is in control and working on your behalf.

Reflection: Are you carrying burdens that you need to surrender to God?

Practical Step: Take 10 minutes to pray and visualize laying your burdens at the feet of Jesus. Picture yourself handing each struggle, one by one, into His capable hands. Write down how you feel afterward. Do you sense peace, relief, or a renewed sense of trust?

Questions:

1. **What does Jesus promise to those who are weary?**

- **Answer:** He promises rest for their souls (Matthew 11:28-30).

2. **Why is it important to rely on God's strength?**

- **Answer:** Our strength is limited, but God's power is perfect and sufficient (2 Corinthians 12:9).

3. **How can resting in God's presence transform your circumstances?**

- **Answer:** Resting in God's presence allows us to find peace and clarity, trusting Him to handle what we cannot.

Declaration Prayer: Heavenly Father, I come to You weary and burdened, seeking Your rest. I release every struggle, every worry, and every fear into Your hands. I trust that You are working all things together for my good. Thank You for being my refuge and strength. I receive Your peace and rest today. In Jesus' name, Amen.

Key Word: Rest

- **Definition:** Spiritual, emotional, and physical peace found through trusting and relying on God's strength instead of our own.

Additional Scripture for Meditation:

- *"Be still, and know that I am God."* — Psalm 46:10

- *"Cast all your anxiety on Him because He cares for you."* — 1 Peter 5:7

Take today to pause, breathe, and lean into God's strength. Allow His rest to renew your soul and empower you for the days ahead.

Day 7:
The Happiness of Your Life Depends on the Quality of Your Thoughts

Focus Scripture: *"Above all else, guard your heart, for everything you do flows from it."* — Proverbs 4:23 (NIV)

Thought Therapy Lesson Your thoughts shape your reality. What you feed your mind determines the quality of your life. Negativity leads to fear, anxiety, and confusion, but focusing on God's Word brings peace, hope, and purpose. Everything in the physical originates in the spiritual, so guard your mind and heart diligently.

When you think thoughts rooted in God's Word, you begin to see yourself and your life through His eyes. Instead of dwelling on failure, frustration, or fear, declare God's truth over your life. His Word is a firm foundation that helps you overcome negativity and experience transformation.

Reflection: Are you feeding your mind with God's truth or with negativity?

Practical Step: Go to a mirror, look at yourself, and declare: *"I praise You, Lord, for I am fearfully and wonderfully made; Your works are wonderful, and I know that full well."* (Psalm 139:14)

Questions:

1. **Why is it important to guard your heart and mind?**

- **Answer:** Everything we do flows from what we think and believe (Proverbs 4:23).

2. **What happens when you focus on God's Word instead of negativity?**

- **Answer:** You experience peace, hope, and clarity.

3. **How can you actively replace negative thoughts?**

- **Answer:** By declaring God's truth and meditating on His promises (Philippians 4:8).

Declaration Prayer: Heavenly Father, I commit my thoughts to You. Help me to guard my heart and feed my mind with Your truth. I choose to focus on Your Word and declare life, hope, and purpose over my circumstances. In Jesus' name, Amen.

Key Word: Guard

- **Definition:** To protect and watch over diligently to prevent harm or negativity.

Additional Scripture for Meditation:

- *"Do not conform to the pattern of this world, but be transformed by the renewing of your mind."* — Romans 12:2

- *"Finally, brothers and sisters, whatever is true, whatever is noble, whatever is right, whatever is pure…think about such things."* — Philippians 4:8

Day 8:
Faith Has It on the Journey

Focus Scripture: *"Even when I walk through the darkest valley, I will not be afraid, for You are close beside me."* — Psalm 23:4 (NLT)

Thought Therapy Lesson Faith is more than a one-time decision; it is a journey that shapes who we are. Even in life's darkest valleys, God is walking with us. The enemy may try to use fear, doubt, or hardship to discourage you, but God promises to turn every situation for good (Genesis 50:20).

Faith is refined in the fire of challenges. These seasons remind us to trust in God's presence and provision. His rod and staff comfort and guide us, giving us strength to take the next step forward.

Reflection: What "dark valleys" are you walking through? How can you trust God to guide you today?

Practical Step: Write down one situation where you feel stuck. Pray and ask God to show you the next step forward in faith, even if it's small.

Questions:

1. **What does Psalm 23:4 teach us about God's presence in trials?**

- **Answer:** God is always with us, even in our darkest moments, to guide and comfort us.

2. **How can hardship strengthen our faith?**

- **Answer:** Hardship teaches us to depend on God's strength and trust His plans.

3. **What promise does Genesis 50:20 offer us?**

- **Answer:** God can turn what the enemy meant for harm into something good.

Declaration Prayer: Lord, I trust in You to guide me through every challenge. Thank You for being my protector, comforter, and helper. I declare that what the enemy meant for evil, You are turning around for my good. In Jesus' name, Amen.

Key Word: Journey

- **Definition:** A continuous process of moving forward in faith with God as our guide.

Additional Scripture for Meditation:

- *"For we walk by faith, not by sight."* — 2 Corinthians 5:7

- *"The Lord Himself goes before you and will be with you; He will never leave you nor forsake you."* — Deuteronomy 31:8

Day 9:
Developing a Positive Vision

Focus Scripture: *"Where there is no vision, the people perish: but he that keepeth the law, happy is he."* — Proverbs 29:18 (KJV)

Thought Therapy Lesson Vision is essential for progress. Without a clear purpose, we wander aimlessly, but God gives us divine revelation to guide our steps. Positive vision fuels faith-filled action, empowering us to fulfill God's plan.

To walk in purpose, we must trust God's direction and move forward, even when circumstances don't make sense. Vision rooted in faith allows us to see beyond today's limitations into tomorrow's possibilities.

Reflection: What vision has God placed in your heart? How can you take a step of faith toward fulfilling it?

Practical Step: Write down your vision and declare: *"Lord, I will fulfill Your plan for my life. I will live with purpose and die empty, having accomplished all You've deposited in me."*

Questions:

1. **What happens when we live without vision?**

- **Answer:** We lack purpose and direction (Proverbs 29:18).

2. **Why is it important to trust God's vision for our lives?**

- **Answer:** God's vision aligns with His perfect plans for us.

3. **How can you take practical steps to pursue God's vision?**

- **Answer:** By seeking His guidance, writing the vision, and walking in obedience (Habakkuk 2:2).

Declaration Prayer: Father, I receive Your vision for my life. I choose to trust and follow Your plan, living a purpose-driven life. Thank You for guiding me with Your divine revelation. In Jesus' name, Amen.

Key Word: Vision

- **Definition:** A clear, God-given purpose and direction that shapes our actions.

Additional Scripture for Meditation:

- *"Write the vision; make it plain on tablets, so he may run who reads it."* — Habakkuk 2:2

- *"Trust in the Lord with all your heart and lean not on your own understanding."* — Proverbs 3:5-6

Day 10:
Stay Focused and Keep Believing

Focus Scripture: *"Do not let your hands be weak, for your work shall be rewarded."* — 2 Chronicles 15:7 (ESV)

Thought Therapy Lesson God calls us to persevere, even when the results seem delayed or invisible. Hard seasons can make it tempting to give up, but every effort made in obedience to God will bring a reward. The work He has assigned to you has purpose, and He promises to strengthen you as you press forward.

When the harvest looks uncertain, trust that God sees every act of faithfulness. Your diligence today is building your breakthrough tomorrow. Stay focused on His promises, for in due season, you will reap a harvest if you do not quit (Galatians 6:9).

Reflection: What work has God called you to that feels unfruitful? How can you remain faithful despite the challenge?

Practical Step: Write down a scripture that encourages perseverance, like Galatians 6:9, and post it somewhere visible to remind yourself to stay faithful.

Questions:

1. **Why does God call us to persevere in challenging seasons?**

- **Answer:** Our faithfulness is an act of trust in God's promises, and He rewards those who endure.

2. **How does Galatians 6:9 encourage you when you feel weary?**

- **Answer:** It reminds us that a harvest is guaranteed if we don't give up.

3. **What practical step can you take today to remain focused on God's work?**

- **Answer:** Lean on God's Word and trust in His perfect timing.

Declaration Prayer: Heavenly Father, I thank You for the work You have entrusted to me. Strengthen me to stay focused, faithful, and determined, knowing that You will reward my efforts in Your perfect timing. I will not grow weary but will press on with hope. In Jesus' name, Amen.

Key Word: Perseverance

- **Definition:** Continued faithfulness and effort despite difficulties or delays.

Additional Scripture for Meditation:

- *"Let us not grow weary of doing good, for in due season we will reap, if we do not give up."* — Galatians 6:9

- *"But as for you, be strong and do not give up, for your work will be rewarded."* — 2 Chronicles 15:7

Day 11:
Faith Changes Everything

Focus Scripture: *"Be joyful in hope, patient in affliction, faithful in prayer."* — Romans 12:12 (NIV)

Thought Therapy Lesson Faith changes our perspective. It reminds us that even in uncertainty, God is faithful. While it's easy to become impatient or doubt during hard times, trust that God's Word never fails. Faith invites us to see God's promises as our reality, even before we experience them.

God's plans are not always aligned with our timing, but they are always perfect. By remaining joyful in hope, patient in affliction, and faithful in prayer, we position ourselves to see His power at work in our lives.

Reflection: Are you trusting God's process, or are you struggling with impatience? How can you surrender your timeline to Him today?

Practical Step: Write a prayer surrendering your timeline and expectations to God. Ask Him for peace and patience as you wait.

Questions:

1. **How does faith change our outlook during challenging seasons?**

- **Answer:** Faith helps us trust God's promises and remain hopeful despite trials.

2. **What does Romans 12:12 teach us about responding to affliction?**

- **Answer:** It encourages us to remain joyful, patient, and prayerful.

3. **Why is prayer essential during seasons of waiting?**

- **Answer:** Prayer aligns our hearts with God's will and strengthens our faith.

Declaration Prayer: Lord, I choose to trust Your timing and remain steadfast in faith. Help me to be joyful in hope, patient in affliction, and faithful in prayer. I believe that Your plans for me are good, and I surrender every worry to You. In Jesus' name, Amen.

Key Word: Faithfulness

- **Definition:** Steadfast trust and commitment to God, regardless of circumstances.

Additional Scripture for Meditation:

- *"Trust in the Lord with all your heart and lean not on your own understanding."* — Proverbs 3:5

- *"We live by faith, not by sight."* — 2 Corinthians 5:7

Day 12:
Nothing Is Too Hard for God

Focus Scripture: *"Ah, Sovereign Lord, You have made the heavens and the earth by Your great power and outstretched arm. Nothing is too hard for You."* — Jeremiah 32:17 (NIV)

Thought Therapy Lesson No challenge is too great for the God who created the universe. Whether you are facing a personal struggle, sickness, or overwhelming odds, remember that God's power knows no limits. What seems impossible to us is entirely possible for Him.

We often limit God with our thinking, but Jeremiah 32:17 reminds us that God's arm is not too short to save. When you surrender your problems to Him, you invite His supernatural power to work on your behalf.

Reflection: What situation in your life feels too big to handle? How can you release it to God and trust in His ability today?

Practical Step: Write down one seemingly impossible situation you are facing. Declare Jeremiah 32:17 over it and trust God to handle it.

Questions:

1. **What does Jeremiah 32:17 teach us about God's power?**

- **Answer:** God's power is unlimited, and nothing is too difficult for Him.

2. **How can you shift your thinking when faced with impossible situations?**

- **Answer:** By focusing on God's promises instead of the problem.

3. **Why is it important to surrender our struggles to God?**

- **Answer:** Surrender allows God's power to work where our strength fails.

Declaration Prayer: Father, I declare that nothing is too hard for You. I release every struggle, worry, and impossible situation into Your hands. I trust in Your power to bring breakthrough and restoration in my life. In Jesus' name, Amen.

Key Word: Sovereign

- **Definition:** Supreme power and authority, fully in control of all things.

Additional Scripture for Meditation:

- *"For with God nothing will be impossible."* — Luke 1:37

- *"Is anything too hard for the Lord?"* — Genesis 18:14

Day 13:
God Turns Nothing Into Something

Focus Scripture: *"Abraham believed in the God who brings the dead back to life and who creates new things out of nothing."* — Romans 4:17 (NLT)

Thought Therapy Lesson When you think you've hit a dead end, remember that God specializes in creating something out of nothing. Abraham trusted God to fulfill His promise when everything seemed impossible. In the same way, God can take your emptiness, loss, or hopeless situation and turn it into a testimony of His faithfulness.

God's resurrection power brings dead dreams back to life. Choose to THINK it, SPEAK it, WRITE it, and WORK it into existence. His Word never returns void.

Reflection: What area of your life feels barren or lifeless? How can you trust God to breathe new life into it?

Practical Step: Write down one promise from God's Word that applies to your situation. Declare it aloud daily.

Questions:

1. **What does Romans 4:17 teach us about God's creative power?**

- **Answer:** God can bring life to dead situations and create new things out of nothing.

2. **Why is it important to trust God when you face a dead end?**

- **Answer:** Trusting God allows His supernatural power to work beyond our limitations.

3. **How can you align your words with God's promises?**

- **Answer:** By declaring His truth over your circumstances and rejecting negativity.

Declaration Prayer: Heavenly Father, I trust You to create something beautiful out of my emptiness. I declare that You are breathing new life into every barren area of my life. I speak Your promises and believe that You will fulfill them. In Jesus' name, Amen.

Key Word: Resurrection

- **Definition:** The act of bringing back to life or restoring what was once dead.

Additional Scripture for Meditation:

- *"I am the resurrection and the life. Anyone who believes in me will live, even after dying."* — John 11:25

- *"Behold, I will do a new thing; now it shall spring forth; shall ye not know it?"* — Isaiah 43:19

Day 14:
Moving Beyond Negativity

Focus Scripture: *"Do not conform to the pattern of this world, but be transformed by the renewing of your mind."* — Romans 12:2 (NIV)

Thought Therapy Lesson Negativity clouds your vision and limits your growth. To break free, you must develop the mind of Christ. When you meditate on God's Word, your thoughts begin to align with His perspective. His thoughts are pure, lovely, and praiseworthy (Philippians 4:8).

Replace negative thoughts with scriptural truth and allow God to transform your mind. This shift will lead to freedom, clarity, and purpose.

Reflection: What negative thoughts are you battling? How can you replace them with God's Word today?

Practical Step: Write down a negative thought and counter it with a scripture. Speak the scripture out loud.

Questions:

1. **Why is renewing your mind essential for spiritual growth?**

- **Answer:** Renewing your mind aligns your thoughts with God's will, leading to transformation.

2. **What happens when you dwell on negative thoughts?**

- **Answer:** Negative thoughts steal joy, hinder growth, and cloud your vision.

3. **How does Philippians 4:8 guide your thinking?**

- **Answer:** It instructs us to focus on what is true, noble, and praiseworthy.

Declaration Prayer: Father, I surrender every negative thought to You. Transform my mind and fill me with Your truth. I choose to meditate on Your Word and reject every lie of the enemy. In Jesus' name, Amen.

Key Word: Renewal

- **Definition:** The process of replacing old patterns of thinking with God's truth.

Additional Scripture for Meditation:

- *"You will keep him in perfect peace, whose mind is stayed on You."* — Isaiah 26:3

- *"As he thinks in his heart, so is he."* — Proverbs 23:7

Day 15:
Waiting on God's Perfect Timing

Focus Scripture: *"Wait for the Lord; be strong and take heart and wait for the Lord."* — Psalm 27:14 (NIV)

Thought Therapy Lesson Waiting is not wasting. In God's waiting room, He is refining you, strengthening you, and aligning you with His plans. Impatience can tempt us to take matters into our own hands, but waiting on God produces renewed strength and trust.

God's timing is always perfect, and He promises to deliver those who wait on Him. Surrender your impatience and trust that His plan is worth the wait.

Reflection: What are you waiting on God for? How can you use this season to grow closer to Him?

Practical Step: Write a prayer of gratitude for this waiting season, trusting that God is working on your behalf.

Questions:

1. **What does Psalm 27:14 teach us about waiting?**

- **Answer:** It encourages us to be strong and trust in God's perfect timing.

2. **Why does God allow waiting seasons?**

- **Answer:** To refine our faith, develop patience, and prepare us for His promises.

3. **How can you remain hopeful while waiting?**

- **Answer:** By focusing on God's faithfulness and His promises.

Declaration Prayer: Lord, I choose to wait on Your perfect timing. I trust that You are working behind the scenes for my good. Strengthen my heart and renew my hope as I rest in Your promises. In Jesus' name, Amen.

Key Word: Patience

- **Definition:** The ability to endure delays with trust, peace, and hope in God.

Additional Scripture for Meditation:

- *"But they that wait upon the Lord shall renew their strength; they shall mount up with wings as eagles."* — Isaiah 40:31

- *"Be still before the Lord and wait patiently for Him."* — Psalm 37:7

Day 16:
God Is Putting an Expiration Date on Your Struggle

Focus Scripture: *"The LORD is close to the brokenhearted and saves those who are crushed in spirit. Many are the afflictions of the righteous, but the LORD delivers him out of them all."* — Psalm 34:18-19 (ESV)

Thought Therapy Lesson Your struggles are not permanent. God has promised to deliver you and turn your trials into testimonies. Every season of pain, delay, and disappointment has an expiration date. Trust in God's perfect timing and His ability to bring beauty from ashes.

Shift your focus from your struggles to God's faithfulness. He is working behind the scenes to turn your adversity into victory and your mess into a message.

Reflection: What struggle in your life feels never-ending? How can you surrender it to God today?

Practical Step: Write a declaration of faith that your current struggles will end in victory. Speak it out daily.

Questions:

1. **What does Psalm 34:19 teach about God's deliverance?**

- **Answer:** Though the righteous face many troubles, God promises to deliver them.

2. **How can you trust that God is placing an expiration date on your struggle?**

- **Answer:** By holding onto His promises of faithfulness and victory.

3. **Why is it important to remain hopeful during trials?**

- **Answer:** Hope keeps us anchored in God's ability to bring breakthrough.

Declaration Prayer: Heavenly Father, I declare that my struggles have an expiration date. I trust You to turn my trials into testimonies and bring beauty from my pain. I stand on Your promise of deliverance. In Jesus' name, Amen.

Key Word: Deliverance

- **Definition:** God's act of rescuing or saving His people from trouble.

Additional Scripture for Meditation:

- *"To appoint unto them that mourn in Zion, to give unto them beauty for ashes."* — Isaiah 61:3

- *"This too shall pass."* — 2 Corinthians 4:17-18

Day 17:
No Problem Too Big for God

Focus Scripture: *"Ah, Sovereign LORD, You have made the heavens and the earth by Your great power and outstretched arm. Nothing is too hard for You."* — Jeremiah 32:17 (NIV)

Thought Therapy Lesson When you face problems that feel overwhelming, remember this truth: Nothing is too hard for God. His power is unlimited, and He delights in showing His faithfulness when the odds seem impossible. Choose to shift your focus from the size of your problem to the greatness of your God.

God specializes in impossible situations and brings restoration, healing, and provision where it seems there is none.

Reflection: What problem in your life feels too big to overcome? How can you trust God with it today?

Practical Step: Write a list of your biggest challenges and declare Jeremiah 32:17 over each one.

Questions:

1. **What does Jeremiah 32:17 reveal about God's power?**

- **Answer:** Nothing is beyond God's ability to handle.

2. **Why is it important to surrender your problems to God?**

- **Answer:** Trusting God allows His supernatural power to work on your behalf.

3. **How can you shift your perspective when facing overwhelming challenges?**

- **Answer:** By focusing on God's promises and His proven faithfulness.

Declaration Prayer: Lord, I surrender every problem to You, knowing that nothing is too hard for You. I trust in Your power to restore, provide, and deliver me from every challenge. In Jesus' name, Amen.

Key Word: Sovereignty

- **Definition:** God's supreme power and authority over all things.

Additional Scripture for Meditation:

- *"With man this is impossible, but with God all things are possible."* — Matthew 19:26

- *"Trust in the LORD with all your heart and lean not on your own understanding."* — Proverbs 3:5

Day 18:
Mix Your Faith with the Word

Focus Scripture: *"So is my word that goes out from my mouth: It will not return to me empty, but will accomplish what I desire."* — Isaiah 55:11 (NIV)

Thought Therapy Lesson Faith is the bridge between God's promises and your reality. When you mix faith with God's Word, you activate the power of His promises in your life. His Word is alive, powerful, and never fails to fulfill its purpose.

To see transformation, you must not only hear God's Word but also believe it and act upon it. Speak His promises over your life daily, aligning your faith with His truth.

Reflection: Are you applying faith to God's Word in your current season? How can you strengthen your faith today?

Practical Step: Choose one promise from God's Word and speak it over your life throughout the day.

Questions:

1. **What does Isaiah 55:11 teach us about God's Word?**

•   **Answer:** It always accomplishes its purpose and never returns empty.

2. **How can you mix faith with God's Word in your daily life?**

•   **Answer:** By declaring His promises, trusting Him, and taking steps of faith.

3. **Why is faith essential for seeing God's promises fulfilled?**

•   **Answer:** Faith activates the power of His Word and aligns our actions with His will.

Declaration Prayer: Father, I mix my faith with Your Word and declare that Your promises will be fulfilled in my life. I trust You to accomplish all that You desire for me. In Jesus' name, Amen.

Key Word: Activation

- **Definition:** The process of putting faith into action by believing and acting on God's Word.

Additional Scripture for Meditation:

- *"Faith without works is dead."* — James 2:26

- *"Let us hold fast the confession of our hope without wavering, for He who promised is faithful."* — Hebrews 10:23

Day 19:
With God by Your Side,
Failure Doesn't Exist

Focus Scripture: *"Consider it pure joy, my brothers and sisters, whenever you face trials of many kinds, because you know that the testing of your faith produces perseverance."* — James 1:2-3 (NIV)

Thought Therapy Lesson Trials are not meant to break you but to build you. When God is on your side, failure is not final. He uses challenges to strengthen your faith, produce perseverance, and prepare you for greater purpose.

Failure only exists when you give up. Trust that God's plan is still unfolding, and every setback is a setup for His divine comeback.

Reflection: How can you shift your perspective and see your challenges as opportunities for growth?

Practical Step: Write a list of past failures and identify how God worked through those situations to bring growth or victory.

Questions:

1. **What does James 1:2-3 teach us about trials?**

- **Answer:** Trials test our faith and produce perseverance for spiritual maturity.

2. **How can failure be part of God's plan?**

- **Answer:** God uses challenges to prepare us for His purpose and strengthen our faith.

3. **Why is perseverance key to overcoming trials?**

- **Answer:** Perseverance helps us endure hardships and move closer to God's promises.

Declaration Prayer: Lord, I thank You for walking with me through every challenge. I declare that with You, failure does not exist. Every trial is building my faith and leading me to victory. In Jesus' name, Amen.

Key Word: Perseverance

- **Definition:** Steadfastness in doing something despite difficulty or delay.

Additional Scripture for Meditation:

- *"I can do all things through Christ who strengthens me."* — Philippians 4:13

- *"For the righteous falls seven times and rises again."* — Proverbs 24:16

Day 20:
Turning Disappointments into Divine Appointments

Focus Scripture: *"So do not fear, for I am with you; do not be dismayed, for I am your God. I will strengthen you and help you; I will uphold you with my righteous right hand."* — Isaiah 41:10 (NIV)

Thought Therapy Lesson Disappointments can feel like closed doors, but they often lead to God's divine appointments. Trust that every setback is an opportunity for God to work His supernatural favor in your life.

When you shift your perspective, you will begin to see God turning what the enemy meant for evil into something good.

Reflection: What disappointment are you facing right now? How can you invite God into this situation?

Practical Step: Write down a disappointment and ask God to show you how He is using it for your good.

Questions:

1. **How does Isaiah 41:10 encourage us in times of disappointment?**

• **Answer:** It reminds us of God's presence, strength, and support.

2. **Why does God allow disappointments?**

• **Answer:** To redirect us toward His purpose and reveal His greater plan.

3. **How can you turn a setback into a testimony?**

• **Answer:** By trusting God's timing and sharing His faithfulness with others.

Declaration Prayer: Father, I give You my disappointments and trust You to turn them into divine appointments. Thank You for working all things for my good. In Jesus' name, Amen.

Key Word: Redemption

- **Definition:** God's act of turning loss or disappointment into something beautiful and purposeful.

Additional Scripture for Meditation:

- *"And we know that in all things God works for the good of those who love Him."* — Romans 8:28

- *"What the enemy meant for evil, God meant for good."* — Genesis 50:20

Day 21:
Expect God to Water Every Barren Area of Your Life

Focus Scripture: *"Sing, O barren, you who have not borne! Enlarge the place of your tent... for you shall expand to the right and to the left."* — Isaiah 54:1-3 (NKJV)

Thought Therapy Lesson God specializes in bringing life to barren places. Even when it seems nothing is growing, trust that He is at work beneath the surface. Your season of barrenness is not permanent; it is preparing the ground for a greater harvest.

Hold onto God's promise to enlarge your territory and bring fruitfulness where there was once dryness.

Reflection: What area of your life feels barren? How can you trust God to bring growth?

Practical Step: Write a prayer thanking God for watering the barren areas of your life and declare fruitfulness over them.

Questions:

1. **What does Isaiah 54:1-3 teach us about barrenness?**

- **Answer:** God turns barrenness into fruitfulness and expands our territory.

2. **How can we trust God in barren seasons?**

- **Answer:** By focusing on His promises and preparing for His blessing.

3. **What steps can you take to enlarge your faith in God's provision?**

- **Answer:** By praying, declaring His Word, and staying expectant for breakthrough.

Declaration Prayer: Lord, I trust You to water every barren area of my life. I declare growth, fruitfulness, and expansion as I wait on Your timing. In Jesus' name, Amen.

Key Word: Fruitfulness

- **Definition:** The state of producing positive results or blessings through God's provision.

Additional Scripture for Meditation:

- *"I am the vine; you are the branches. If you remain in me... you will bear much fruit."* — John 15:5

- *"The desert and the parched land will be glad; the wilderness will rejoice and blossom."* — Isaiah 35:1

Day 22:
Unlimited Abundance Awaits You

Focus Scripture: *"The LORD will open the heavens, the storehouse of His bounty, to send rain on your land in season and to bless all the work of your hands."* — Deuteronomy 28:12 (NIV)

Thought Therapy Lesson God's plan for you is not lack but abundance. He is a God of overflow, and His blessings are unlimited. Trust Him to open doors of opportunity, provision, and favor as you remain faithful.

When you align your life with His Word, you position yourself to receive His abundance.

Reflection: Are you living with a mindset of abundance or scarcity? How can you align your thinking with God's promises?

Practical Step: Write down three areas of your life where you need God's abundant provision and pray over them daily.

Questions:

1. **What does Deuteronomy 28:12 teach us about God's blessings?**

- **Answer:** God promises to bless our work and provide abundantly.

2. **How does faith activate God's abundance in our lives?**

- **Answer:** Faith positions us to receive His promises and provision.

3. **What steps can you take to live in expectation of God's abundance?**

- **Answer:** By declaring His promises, sowing seeds of faith, and trusting His timing.

Declaration Prayer: Father, I declare that Your abundance flows in every area of my life. I trust You to open the storehouse of heaven and bless me beyond measure. In Jesus' name, Amen.

Key Word: Abundance

* **Definition:** God's provision that exceeds our needs and overflows into blessings for others.

Additional Scripture for Meditation:

* *"I have come that they may have life, and have it to the full."* — John 10:10

* *"Give, and it will be given to you... a good measure, pressed down, shaken together, and running over."* — Luke 6:38

Day 23:
A Mentality of Abundance

Focus Scripture: *"Forgetting those things which are behind, and reaching forth unto those things which are before, I press toward the mark for the prize of the high calling of God in Christ Jesus."* — Philippians 3:13–14 (KJV)

Thought Therapy Lesson Your mindset determines your future. A mentality of abundance starts with recognizing God's limitless resources and rejecting scarcity thinking. Forget the past failures and hindrances and focus on pressing toward what God has promised. The supernatural increase of God will flow when you align your mind with His Word and expectations.

- **Reflection:** What past failures or setbacks do you need to let go of to embrace abundance?

- **Practical Step:** Write down three blessings you believe God is releasing in your life and declare them daily.

Questions:

1. **How does focusing on the future help you overcome past limitations?**

- **Answer:** It redirects your mind to God's promises and gives you renewed hope (Philippians 3:13).

2. **Why is it important to align your mind with God's abundance?**

- **Answer:** It positions you to receive His increase and supernatural provision (Ephesians 3:20).

3. **What can you do daily to maintain an abundant mindset?**

- **Answer:** Speak life-giving affirmations rooted in God's Word.

Declaration Prayer: Father, I choose to let go of my past and embrace the abundant life You have for me. I press forward with faith and trust that You are releasing supernatural increase and favor over my life. In Jesus' name, Amen.

Day 24:
God's Plans Are Sure and Faithful

Focus Scripture: *"For I know the plans I have for you, declares the Lord, plans to prosper you and not to harm you, plans to give you a hope and a future."* — Jeremiah 29:11 (NIV)

Thought Therapy Lesson God's plans for your life are unshakable, no matter the trials or setbacks. His promises are true and faithful, and He is always working for your good (Romans 8:28). Trust in His purpose, even when the path is unclear, because His plans lead to hope, prosperity, and a future filled with His goodness.

- **Reflection:** Are you trusting in God's plan or relying on your own understanding?

- **Practical Step:** Write a letter of surrender to God, thanking Him for His faithful plans and giving Him control over your future.

Questions:

1. **What does it mean that God's plans are not to harm you but to prosper you?**

- **Answer:** It means His intentions are always for your ultimate good and growth.

2. **How can Romans 8:28 encourage you during challenges?**

- **Answer:** It assures us that God uses every situation to fulfill His purpose.

3. **How do you align yourself with God's plans?**

- **Answer:** By prayer, studying His Word, and yielding your desires to Him.

Declaration Prayer: Lord, I trust Your plans for me. Even when I don't understand, I know Your ways are higher and Your purpose for me is good. I surrender my future to You and walk in faith. In Jesus' name, Amen.

Day 25:
Nothing Too Hard for God

Focus Scripture: *"Ah, Sovereign Lord, You have made the heavens and the earth by Your great power and outstretched arm. Nothing is too hard for You."* — Jeremiah 32:17 (NIV)

Thought Therapy Lesson No challenge is too great, no problem too complex for God. What seems impossible to you is possible with Him. Trust His strength, not your own. He has the power to turn hopeless situations into victories.

- **Reflection:** What is one "impossible" area in your life that you need to surrender to God?

- **Practical Step:** Write a prayer of trust, declaring Jeremiah 32:17 over your situation.

Questions:

1. **Why is it important to remember God's power during hard times?**

- **Answer:** It shifts our focus from our limitations to His unlimited strength.

2. **What happens when we surrender "impossible" situations to God?**

- **Answer:** He begins to work miracles in His perfect timing (Luke 18:27).

3. **How can you practically remind yourself of God's power daily?**

- **Answer:** Meditate on scriptures like Jeremiah 32:17 and Philippians 4:13.

Declaration Prayer: Heavenly Father, nothing is too hard for You. I place my impossible situations in Your hands and trust in Your power to overcome every obstacle. You are my strength and deliverer. In Jesus' name, Amen.

Day 26:
Nothing Is Random with God

Focus Scripture: *"The Lord has established His throne in the heavens, and His kingdom rules over all."* — Psalm 103:19 (ESV)

Thought Therapy Lesson Every event in your life is woven into God's greater plan. Even when life seems scattered or painful, trust that God is sovereign and nothing is random. He works all things for His glory and your good.

- **Reflection:** Do you believe that God is working in every detail of your life?

- **Practical Step:** Write down one area of your life that feels uncertain. Ask God to help you see His purpose in it.

Questions:

1. **How does Psalm 103:19 remind us of God's sovereignty?**

- **Answer:** It affirms that God rules over everything and nothing happens outside His control.

2. **Why is it comforting to know that nothing is random with God?**

- **Answer:** It assures us that every experience has a purpose in His plan.

3. **How can you trust God in times of uncertainty?**

- **Answer:** By meditating on His promises and surrendering your fears to Him.

Declaration Prayer: Lord, I trust in Your sovereignty and perfect plan. Nothing is random in my life because You are in control. I surrender my uncertainties to You and choose to walk in faith. In Jesus' name, Amen.

Day 27:
The Joy of the Lord Is Your Strength

Focus Scripture: *"Do not grieve, for the joy of the Lord is your strength."* — Nehemiah 8:10 (NIV)

Thought Therapy Lesson Joy is more than a feeling; it is a source of strength that comes from God. Even in difficult seasons, the joy of the Lord can sustain you. Lean into His presence, and let His joy renew and strengthen you.

- **Reflection:** What is robbing your joy today, and how can you reclaim it through God's strength?
- **Practical Step:** Take time to worship God today. Thank Him for His joy and strength in your life.

Questions:

1. **Why is the joy of the Lord so powerful?**

- **Answer:** It sustains and strengthens us in every circumstance.

2. **How can you find joy in difficult seasons?**

- **Answer:** By focusing on God's presence and His promises.

3. **What practical steps can you take to cultivate joy daily?**

- **Answer:** Worship, prayer, gratitude, and time in God's Word.

Declaration Prayer: Father, I receive Your joy as my strength. I choose to focus on You and trust that Your joy will carry me through every trial. Thank You for being my source of renewal. In Jesus' name, Amen.

Day 28:
A Season of Unprecedented Favor

Focus Scripture: *"Yes indeed, it won't be long now... Blessings like wine pouring off the mountains and hills."* — Amos 9:13 (MSG)

Thought Therapy Lesson God is releasing a season of favor and acceleration. What seemed delayed will now come quickly. Align your mind and expectations with His Word and prepare to receive His supernatural blessings.

- **Reflection:** Are you ready to receive the favor God has prepared for you?

- **Practical Step:** Write down specific areas where you are expecting God's favor and declare Amos 9:13 over them.

Questions:

1. **What does it mean to walk in God's favor?**

- **Answer:** It means experiencing God's blessings, opportunities, and acceleration.

2. **How can you prepare for God's favor in your life?**

- **Answer:** By praying, expecting, and aligning your thoughts with His Word.

3. **What happens when we trust God's timing?**

- **Answer:** We receive blessings in due season (Galatians 6:9).

Declaration Prayer: Lord, I thank You for this season of unprecedented favor. I align my mind and heart with Your Word and receive the blessings You have prepared for me. In Jesus' name, Amen.

Day 29:
Be Strong and Courageous

Focus Scripture: *"Be strong and courageous. Do not be afraid or terrified because of them, for the LORD your God goes with you; he will never leave you nor forsake you."* — Deuteronomy 31:6 (NIV)

Thought Therapy Lesson Courage comes from trusting God's promises and His presence. Fear seeks to paralyze, but God's Word empowers us to act in boldness. When you stand on God's truth, no situation can overwhelm you. Let courage lead you forward, knowing God goes with you every step of the way.

- **Reflection:** What fear or challenge is holding you back today? How can you step forward in faith?

- **Practical Step:** Write down three affirmations based on God's promises. Speak them aloud when fear arises. Example: "I am not alone; God is with me (Isaiah 41:10)."

Questions:

1. **Why is it important to be courageous in the face of fear?**

- **Answer**: Courage enables us to trust God's plan and fulfill His purpose (Joshua 1:9).

2. **How does God's presence bring comfort in difficult situations?**

- **Answer**: His presence assures us of protection and strength (Psalm 23:4).

3. **What promise does Deuteronomy 31:6 hold for believers?**

- **Answer**: God will never leave us or forsake us, even in trials.

Declaration Prayer Heavenly Father, I choose to be strong and courageous because I know You are with me. I cast out fear and step forward in faith, trusting Your promises. Thank You for never leaving me. In Jesus' name, Amen.

Key Word: Courage

- *Definition:* The ability to act in faith despite fear, knowing God's presence sustains you.

Additional Scriptures for Meditation:

- Joshua 1:9

- Isaiah 41:10

- Psalm 27:1

Day 30:
God Will Turn It Around

Focus Scripture: *"And we know that in all things God works for the good of those who love him, who have been called according to his purpose."* — Romans 8:28 (NIV)

Thought Therapy Lesson What the enemy means for harm, God uses for good. Your trials, disappointments, and struggles are not wasted. God is always working behind the scenes to turn every situation around for your good and His glory.

- **Reflection:** What current challenge can you trust God to use for good?

- **Practical Step:** Write down one area where you've faced disappointment. Declare: "God is turning this around for my good."

Questions:

1. **What does Romans 8:28 teach us about God's plans?**

- **Answer**: God works all things—even hardships—for the good of those who love Him.

2. **How can we trust God when situations seem hopeless?**

- **Answer**: By remembering His faithfulness and promises (Genesis 50:20).

3. **How does focusing on God's purpose shift our perspective?**

- **Answer**: It allows us to see trials as opportunities for growth and transformation.

Declaration Prayer Father, I thank You that You are working all things for my good. What the enemy meant for evil, You are turning around for my victory. I trust Your plan and purpose for my life. In Jesus' name, Amen.

Key Word: Restoration

- *Definition:* The act of God taking what is broken or lost and transforming it for His glory and our good.

Additional Scriptures for Meditation:

- Genesis 50:20

- Isaiah 61:3

- 2 Corinthians 4:17

Day 31:
Accentuate the Positive

Focus Scripture: *"Finally, brothers and sisters, whatever is true, whatever is noble, whatever is right, whatever is pure, whatever is lovely, whatever is admirable—if anything is excellent or praiseworthy—think about such things."* — Philippians 4:8 (NIV)

Thought Therapy Lesson Your mindset determines your outlook. When you focus on the good in your life, you cultivate gratitude, joy, and peace. Shift your thoughts away from negativity and focus on the truth and beauty of God's Word.

- **Reflection:** Are your thoughts more positive or negative? How can you refocus them on God's goodness?

- **Practical Step:** Write down five positive things in your life. Thank God for each one today.

Questions:

1. **Why is it important to focus on what is pure and praiseworthy?**

- **Answer**: It aligns our minds with God's truth and produces peace (Philippians 4:9).

2. **How does gratitude transform our thoughts?**

- **Answer:** Gratitude shifts our focus from problems to God's provision.

3. **What practical steps can help us change our thought patterns?**

- **Answer**: Speaking God's Word and focusing on His promises.

Declaration Prayer Lord, I choose to focus on what is true, noble, and praiseworthy. I reject negativity and embrace the peace that comes from aligning my thoughts with Your Word. In Jesus' name, Amen.

Key Word: Mindset

- *Definition:* The established set of attitudes and beliefs that shape how you think and act.

Additional Scriptures for Meditation:

- Colossians 3:2

- Isaiah 26:3

- Romans 12:2

Day 32:
Trusting God's Timing

Focus Scripture: *"But do not forget this one thing, dear friends: With the Lord a day is like a thousand years, and a thousand years are like a day."* — 2 Peter 3:8 (NIV)

Thought Therapy Lesson God's timing is perfect, even when it doesn't match our expectations. Waiting on the Lord teaches us patience, trust, and reliance on His wisdom. Delay does not mean denial—God is always at work.

- **Reflection:** Are you struggling to wait on God's timing? What can you learn during this season?

- **Practical Step:** Write a prayer surrendering your timeline to God. Trust Him to fulfill His promises.

Questions:

1. **How does God's timing differ from ours?**

- **Answer:** God operates outside of human time; He sees the full picture (Isaiah 55:8-9).

2. **Why is waiting on God beneficial?**

- **Answer:** It builds trust, patience, and spiritual maturity (James 1:4).

3. **What does it mean to trust God fully with your plans?**

- **Answer**: It means surrendering control and believing in His perfect will.

Declaration Prayer Father, I trust Your timing in all things. Teach me patience and help me surrender my plans to You. I believe You are working all things for my good. In Jesus' name, Amen.

Key Word: Patience

- *Definition:* The ability to endure delay and trust in God's perfect timing.

Additional Scriptures for Meditation:

- Isaiah 40:31

- Ecclesiastes 3:1

- Habakkuk 2:3

Day 33:
Trust God's Timing

Focus Scripture: *"But do not forget this one thing, dear friends: With the Lord a day is like a thousand years, and a thousand years are like a day."* — 2 Peter 3:8 (NIV)

Thought Therapy Lesson God's timing is perfect, even when it feels delayed. Trust that He is never late. When we try to rush His process, we cause unnecessary worry. Instead, focus on seeking His kingdom first and trust that all things will align in their season (Matthew 6:33).

- **Reflection:** Are you struggling to wait on God's timing? What can you surrender to Him today?

- **Practical Step:** Write a letter to God expressing your trust in His timing. End with a declaration of faith.

Questions

1. **What does 2 Peter 3:8 teach us about God's view of time?**

Answer: God's perspective of time is eternal; He is not bound by our limited understanding.

2. **How does seeking God's kingdom first impact your ability to trust His timing?**

Answer: It shifts our focus from anxiety to His provision and promises.

3. **What can you do while waiting on God's promises?**

Answer: Pray, worship, and remain obedient to His Word.

Declaration Prayer Heavenly Father, I trust Your perfect timing. I surrender my impatience and my timeline to You. I know that You are working all things together for my good. In Jesus' name, Amen.

Key Word: *Timing*

Definition: God's appointed time for His plans to unfold perfectly in our lives.

Additional Scriptures for Meditation:

- Ecclesiastes 3:11

- Isaiah 40:31

- Psalm 27:14

Day 34:
Do Not Let Fear Rule Your Life

Focus Scripture: *"For God has not given us a spirit of fear, but of power and of love and of a sound mind."* — 2 Timothy 1:7 (NKJV)

Thought Therapy Lesson Fear is not from God. When we let fear take control, we forfeit the power and peace He has given us. Fear cripples us, but faith empowers us. Today, replace fear with the promises of God and step into His peace.

- **Reflection:** What fears are holding you back? How can you surrender them to God?

- **Practical Step:** Write down one fear and a scripture that counters it. Declare the scripture out loud.

Questions

1. **What spirit has God given us in place of fear?**

Answer: A spirit of power, love, and a sound mind.

2. **Why is fear not from God?**

Answer: Fear opposes the nature of God and His promises.

3. **How can faith overcome fear in your life?**

Answer: By focusing on God's Word and trusting in His power.

Declaration Prayer Father, I reject the spirit of fear and embrace Your power, love, and peace. I declare that fear has no hold over my life because I trust in You. In Jesus' name, Amen.

Key Word: *Fear*

Definition: A paralyzing emotion that does not align with God's nature or promises.

Additional Scriptures for Meditation:

- Isaiah 41:10

- Psalm 23:4

- Romans 8:15

Day 35:
God Turns Brokenness into Beauty

Focus Scripture: *"To appoint unto them that mourn in Zion, to give unto them beauty for ashes, the oil of joy for mourning, the garment of praise for the spirit of heaviness."* — Isaiah 61:3 (KJV)

Thought Therapy Lesson God specializes in turning broken situations into something beautiful. Your pain, failures, and disappointments are not the end of your story. Trust God to bring beauty out of ashes and to use your brokenness for His glory.

- **Reflection:** What broken area in your life needs God's healing touch today?

- **Practical Step:** Write a prayer inviting God to bring beauty into an area where you feel broken.

Questions

1. **How does Isaiah 61:3 encourage us during seasons of brokenness?**

Answer: It reminds us that God can bring joy and beauty out of sorrow.

2. **What is the significance of "beauty for ashes"?**

Answer: It symbolizes God's ability to redeem and transform painful situations.

3. **How can you praise God in the midst of a difficult season?**

Answer: By focusing on His promises and worshiping Him for who He is.

Declaration Prayer Lord, I thank You for turning my brokenness into beauty. I trust You to redeem my pain and bring joy into my life. I praise You for Your faithfulness. In Jesus' name, Amen.

Key Word: *Beauty*

Definition: God's ability to bring restoration, joy, and purpose out of pain and brokenness.

Additional Scriptures for Meditation:

- Romans 8:28

- Psalm 147:3

- 2 Corinthians 12:9

Day 36:
Keep Your Eyes on Jesus

Focus Scripture: *"Fixing our eyes on Jesus, the pioneer and perfecter of faith."* — Hebrews 12:2 (NIV)

Thought Therapy Lesson Distractions and challenges can cause us to lose focus, but when we fix our eyes on Jesus, He gives us the strength to persevere. Jesus is the author and finisher of our faith, and keeping Him at the center brings clarity and direction.

- **Reflection:** What distractions are pulling your focus away from Jesus?

- **Practical Step:** Take 5 minutes to pray, refocus, and invite Jesus to center your thoughts.

Questions

1. **Why is it important to fix our eyes on Jesus?**

Answer: He is the source of our strength and the perfecter of our faith.

2. **What happens when we allow distractions to take our focus off Him?**

Answer: We lose clarity, peace, and direction.

3. **How can you realign your focus on Jesus daily?**

Answer: Through prayer, worship, and meditation on His Word.

Declaration Prayer Jesus, I fix my eyes on You. I surrender every distraction and trust You to guide me. You are the author and perfecter of my faith. I will keep my focus on You alone. In Your name, Amen.

Key Word: *Focus*

Definition: Intentional concentration on Jesus, removing distractions to trust in His direction and promises.

Additional Scriptures for Meditation:

- Colossians 3:2

- Matthew 14:29-31

- Psalm 16:8

Day 37:
God Will Restore What Was Lost

Focus Scripture: *"I will repay you for the years the locusts have eaten... You will have plenty to eat, until you are full, and you will praise the name of the Lord your God."* — Joel 2:25-26 (NIV)

Thought Therapy Lesson God is a God of restoration. What the enemy stole, what time seemed to waste, or what sin caused to be lost can be restored by God. He can multiply what was taken and give you a greater harvest than before. Trust Him to repay and renew your life in miraculous ways.

- **Reflection:** What areas in your life feel lost or stolen? How can you invite God's restoration?

- **Practical Step:** Write a list of what you feel has been lost and pray, asking God to restore and renew those areas.

Questions

1. **What does Joel 2:25 teach us about God's nature?**

Answer: He is a restorer, capable of redeeming lost time and blessings.

2. **How can we hold on to hope when we experience loss?**

Answer: By trusting God's promises and believing in His faithfulness.

3. **What steps can you take to partner with God's plan of restoration in your life?**

Answer: Pray, trust, and act in faith while focusing on God's Word.

Declaration Prayer Heavenly Father, I thank You for being a God of restoration. I believe that what has been lost will be repaid, multiplied, and renewed in my life. I trust You to bring beauty and blessing out of what seemed broken. In Jesus' name, Amen.

Key Word: *Restoration*

Definition: The act of returning something to its original or better condition through God's grace and power.

Additional Scriptures for Meditation:

- Job 42:10

- Isaiah 61:7

- 1 Peter 5:10

Day 38:
Walk by Faith, Not by Sight

Focus Scripture: *"For we walk by faith, not by sight."* — 2 Corinthians 5:7 (NKJV)

Thought Therapy Lesson Faith often requires us to move forward without seeing the full picture. It's about trusting God when the path seems unclear. Do not be discouraged by what you see in the natural. God's promises are already in motion, even if you can't see them yet.

- **Reflection:** Are you struggling to trust God because you can't see the outcome? How can you strengthen your faith?

- **Practical Step:** Write down one area where you need to trust God more fully. Declare out loud: "I will walk by faith and not by sight."

Questions

1. **What does it mean to walk by faith and not by sight?**

Answer: To trust in God's promises and guidance, even when we can't see the outcome.

2. **Why is faith essential to the Christian life?**

Answer: It connects us to God's promises and allows us to trust Him beyond circumstances.

3. **How can you strengthen your faith in uncertain times?**

Answer: Through prayer, studying the Word, and recalling past testimonies.

Declaration Prayer Lord, I choose to walk by faith and not by sight. I trust that Your promises are true, even when I cannot see the outcome. I declare that my faith is growing stronger in You. In Jesus' name, Amen.

Key Word: *Faith*

Definition: Complete trust in God's promises, even without visible proof or immediate results.

Additional Scriptures for Meditation:

- Hebrews 11:1
- Romans 10:17
- James 1:3-4

Day 39:
God Is Working Behind the Scenes

Focus Scripture: *"And we know that in all things God works for the good of those who love Him, who have been called according to His purpose."* — Romans 8:28 (NIV)

Thought Therapy Lesson Even when it feels like nothing is happening, God is at work behind the scenes. He is orchestrating details, aligning people, and preparing blessings that you can't yet see. Trust that He is faithful to complete what He has started in your life.

- **Reflection:** Can you recall a time when God worked behind the scenes for your good? How does that encourage you today?

- **Practical Step:** Write a list of current struggles and declare: "God is working this for my good."

Questions

1. **What does Romans 8:28 teach us about God's plans for our lives?**

Answer: God works all things, even challenges, for our good when we trust Him.

2. **Why is it important to trust God when we don't see immediate results?**

Answer: His timing and ways are perfect, even when we don't understand.

3. **How can you stay encouraged while waiting on God's plans to unfold?**

Answer: By praying, meditating on His Word, and remembering His faithfulness.

Declaration Prayer Father, I thank You for working all things for my good. Even when I cannot see it, I trust that You are behind the scenes aligning every detail for my purpose. I rest in Your faithfulness. In Jesus' name, Amen.

Key Word: *Providence*

Definition: God's divine care, guidance, and provision in every detail of life.

Additional Scriptures for Meditation:

- Philippians 1:6

- Isaiah 64:4

- Psalm 37:23

Day 40:
Step into Your Promise

Focus Scripture: *"Every place that the sole of your foot will tread upon I have given to you, just as I promised to Moses."* — Joshua 1:3 (ESV)

Thought Therapy Lesson God has promises for your life, but you must step out in faith to receive them. Don't let fear, doubt, or past failures hold you back. Be strong and courageous, knowing that where God calls you, He will provide and protect.

- **Reflection:** What promise has God given you that you need to step into?

- **Practical Step:** Write down one bold step of faith you will take today to pursue God's promise.

Questions

1. **What does Joshua 1:3 teach us about stepping into God's promises?**

Answer: God gives us territory, but we must take action in faith.

2. **How can fear hold us back from God's plans?**

Answer: Fear causes us to doubt God's provision and power.

3. **What step of faith do you need to take to see God's promises fulfilled?**

Answer: Obedience, prayer, and trust in His Word.

Declaration Prayer Lord, I step boldly into the promises You have prepared for me. I refuse to let fear or doubt hold me back. I declare that every step I take is guided by Your Word, and I will possess the land You have given me. In Jesus' name, Amen.

Key Word: *Promise*

Definition: God's declared intention to provide blessings, fulfill His plans, and remain faithful to His Word.

Additional Scriptures for Meditation:

- Joshua 1:9

- Deuteronomy 31:6

- Hebrews 10:23

Glossary of Key Terms

1. Prophetic Thinking: A mindset focused on aligning one's thoughts with God's promises and higher ways.

2. Thought Therapy: The process of renewing the mind by replacing negative thoughts with God's truth.

3. Transformation: A complete change in one's thoughts, actions, and character to align with God's will (Romans 12:2).

4. Declaration Prayer: A prayer that boldly proclaims God's promises over one's life.

5. Faith: The confidence to trust in God's plans and promises even without seeing immediate results (Hebrews 11:1).

6. Renewal: The process of becoming spiritually revived and aligned with God's Word (Isaiah 40:31).

7. Possibility Thinking: Seeing beyond circumstances and trusting God to do the impossible (Ephesians 3:20).

Prophetic Prayers for Transformation

1. **Prayer for Renewing the Mind:**

Lord, I surrender my thoughts to You. Replace every negative thought with Your truth. Help me to meditate on what is pure, lovely, and praiseworthy. Transform me by the renewing of my mind. In Jesus' name, Amen.

2. **Prayer for Trusting God's Process:**

Father, I trust Your timing and Your ways. Help me to release my impatience and fully surrender to Your plan. Strengthen my faith as I wait on You. In Jesus' name, Amen.

3. **Prayer for Speaking Life:**

Lord, let my words align with Your promises. Teach me to speak life over my circumstances and declare victory in every situation. In Jesus' name, Amen.

4. **Prayer for Walking in Purpose:**

Heavenly Father, guide my steps and give me the boldness to walk in the purpose You have called me to. Help me to trust in Your power and provision. In Jesus' name, Amen.

Bonus Sections 1-4

Section 1: Renewing Your Mindset

Scripture Focus: Romans 12:2 – "Do not conform to the pattern of this world, but be transformed by the renewing of your mind. Then you will be able to test and approve what God's will is—his good, pleasing and perfect will."

Reflective Questions with Examples

1. **What recurring thoughts or beliefs are holding you back from trusting God completely?**

- Example: *"I always think I'm not good enough to succeed in my calling."*

2. **How does the way you think impact your decisions and actions in daily life?**

- Example: *"When I doubt my abilities, I avoid opportunities that require leadership because I feel unqualified."*

3. **What truths from God's Word can replace negative or limiting thoughts?**

- Example: *Replace "I am not good enough" with Philippians 4:13 – "I can do all things through Christ who strengthens me."*

Exercise: Mindset Renewal Journal with Examples

1. **Write down 3 limiting thoughts or lies you've believed about yourself.**

- Example:
- *Lie 1:* "I will always fail."
- *Lie 2:* "God doesn't care about my struggles."
- *Lie 3:* "I can never change."

2. **Find a corresponding scripture that counters each lie with God's truth.**

- Example:

- *Truth for Lie 1:* Joshua 1:9 – "Be strong and courageous. Do not be afraid; do not be discouraged, for the Lord your God will be with you wherever you go."

- *Truth for Lie 2:* 1 Peter 5:7 – "Cast all your anxiety on Him because He cares for you."

- *Truth for Lie 3:* 2 Corinthians 5:17 – "Therefore, if anyone is in Christ, the new creation has come: The old has gone, the new is here!"

3. **Declare these truths daily for 7 days and document any changes.**

- Example Journal Entry:

- *Day 1:* "I felt a shift today when I spoke Joshua 1:9 aloud before my meeting. I felt more confident and prepared."

- *Day 2:* "I reminded myself that God cares for me, and it helped me trust Him with my financial concerns."

Section 2: Thriving in Ministry

Scripture Focus: Joshua 1:8 – "Keep this Book of the Law always on your lips; meditate on it day and night, so that you may be careful to do everything written in it. Then you will be prosperous and successful."

Reflective Questions with Examples

1. **How does your thought life influence your effectiveness in ministry?**

- Example: *"When I think I'm not making a difference, I hesitate to share the Word boldly."*

2. **Are there areas where fear or doubt have hindered your ministry goals?**

- Example: *"I've avoided leading a Bible study because I fear I don't know enough Scripture to answer questions."*

3. **What is one area where you feel God is calling you to step out in faith?**

- Example: *"I believe God is calling me to mentor younger believers, but I'm unsure how to start."*

Exercise: Ministry Vision Plan with Examples

1. **Write down your ministry's mission and vision statement.**

- Example: *"Mission: To empower believers to grow in faith and walk in God's purpose. Vision: To build a community of Christ-centered individuals impacting the world for God's glory."*

2. **Identify three areas where your ministry can grow or improve.**

- Example:
- *1. Outreach to the local community.*
- *2. Improving discipleship programs.*
- *3. Developing better communication strategies.*

3. **Create an action plan for one of these areas.**

- Example:
- *Goal:* Outreach to the local community.
- *Prayer Point:* Ask God for wisdom and provision for community outreach.
- *Steps:*

1. Partner with local shelters to host monthly events.

2. Gather volunteers and resources for outreach.

3. Share testimonies during Sunday services to inspire involvement.

Section 3: Marketplace Success God's Way

Scripture Focus: Proverbs 16:3 – "Commit to the Lord whatever you do, and he will establish your plans."

Reflective Questions with Examples

1. **What are your goals in the marketplace, and how do they align with God's purpose for your life?**

- Example: *"I want to grow my business to provide jobs in my community, reflecting God's love through service."*

2. **How can you incorporate biblical principles into your business practices?**

- Example: *"I will practice integrity by being honest in all financial transactions (Proverbs 11:1)."*

3. **What fears or doubts do you need to overcome to step into your full potential in the marketplace?**

- Example: *"I fear taking risks, but I will trust God to guide my decisions."*

Exercise: Marketplace Alignment with Examples

1. **Write down your top three business or career goals.**

- Example:

- *1. Launch a new product line by next quarter.*

- *2. Increase customer satisfaction through personalized service.*

- *3. Expand outreach by partnering with faith-based organizations.*

2. **Identify a biblical principle or scripture that supports each goal.**

- Example:

- *Goal 1:* Philippians 4:19 – "And my God will meet all your needs according to the riches of His glory in Christ Jesus."

- *Goal 2:* Colossians 3:23 – "Whatever you do, work at it with all your heart, as working for the Lord."

- *Goal 3:* Ecclesiastes 4:9 – "Two are better than one, because they have a good return for their labor."

3. **Create a plan to implement these principles into your daily work.**

- Example:

- *Goal:* Increase customer satisfaction.

- *Plan:* Conduct weekly team meetings to discuss feedback and improvements. Pray over each meeting for wisdom.

Section 4: Integrating Mindset, Ministry, and Marketplace

Scripture Focus: Colossians 3:23-24 – "Whatever you do, work at it with all your heart, as working for the Lord, not for human masters."

Reflective Questions with Examples

1. **How do your mindset, ministry, and marketplace roles influence one another?**

- Example: *"When my mindset is aligned with God, I feel more confident in both ministry and business."*

2. **What steps can you take to ensure that your thinking in all three areas aligns with God's Word?**

- Example: *"I will set aside time each morning to meditate on Scripture and pray for guidance in all areas of my life."*

3. **How does success in these areas glorify God and serve others?**

- Example: *"By succeeding in my business, I can provide resources for my ministry and support missions work."*

Closing Encouragement

Congratulations! You have completed **40 Days of Thought Therapy**. Remember that this is not the end of your journey but the beginning of a transformed mindset. Continue to meditate on God's Word, declare His promises daily, and walk boldly in faith. God has great plans for your life—plans to prosper you, give you hope, and ensure a victorious future (Jeremiah 29:11).

You are fearfully and wonderfully made.

You are strong, courageous, and victorious.

You are a child of God, destined for greatness.

Keep thinking God's way and watch Him revolutionize your life!

www.ingramcontent.com/pod-product-compliance
Lightning Source LLC
Chambersburg PA
CBHW051541120626
46551CB00013B/1321